Doing Business Like a Fighter Pilot

G Suit and Helmet Not Required

Phil Brewer

DOING BUSINESS LIKE A FIGHTER PILOT: G SUIT AND HELMET NOT REQUIRED
Phil Brewer

Original edition printed 2011
Second edition printed 2019

www.philbrewer.com
phil@philbrewer.com

ISBN-10: 0615527000
ISBN-13: 978-0615527000

"When you have tasted flight, you will forever walk the earth with your eyes turned skyward, for there you have been, and there you will always long to return."

Leonardo da Vinci

"As a fully qualified A-7D pilot, Phil Brewer came into the 353 Tactical Fighter Squadron at Myrtle Beach AFB which I commanded over four decades ago. We had a most interesting and challenging mission involving all aspects of attack fighter flying, from interdiction to Close Air Support, with every conventional weapon, and we did Search and Rescue training. We had frequent opportunities to participate in the realistic combat training in the Red Flag program.

I can certainly vouch that Phil knows whereof he speaks in this aptly named volume, <u>G-Suit and Helmet Not Required</u>—not required for the reading but central to the writing! His comments in *About Pilots* are absolutely true, and his take away advice which follows is, in my view, exactly on target—the target of a rewarding and exemplary life.

Phil had many amazing subsequent experiences after Myrtle Beach in the air—military and civilian and as a business man. I discovered his lessons on life and its meaning when we met again at an A-7D pilot reunion in 2018. They are well worth reading and reflecting."

Gary R. Tompkins, Colonel USAF (Ret.)

"In a world that presents so many challenges to overcome, Phil is a voice of clarity, wisdom, and faith. Recognizing that everything required to face—and conquer—the challenges of life is already inside of us, G Suit and Helmet Not Required takes the reader on a journey to unlock the gifts God has given each of us. Though seemingly insignificant at first glance, the steps of doing fighter pilot-style business provide a framework for serious business success. The process encourages commitment to small wins, finding a healthy environment to flourish in, and learning master and domination in your sector . . . all to push forward and repeat the cycle! G Suit has inspired me to place my focus in the right place so that I might be a better man, Christian, husband, father and priest."

V.Rev. Fr. Christopher Salamy – Pastor, St. George Antiochian Orthodox

Church, Phoenix, Arizona

This book is dedicated to all the people in my life who have been instrumental in my business and professional success. Many of you were my teachers. Many were my mentor students. All of you played a part.

I wish to acknowledge the incredible work by my editor, Rachel J. Beard, who worked with me on countless rewrites and editions. The readability of this finished work was only possible through her very talented grasp of the intricacies.

One day, I thought it would be fun to take my then young son to the Pima Air Museum in Tucson, Arizona. I proudly showed him the four airplanes that I had piloted while on active duty in the USAF. Three of those four planes in the museum were even the very plane I had flown. A few seconds of silence ensued. Then, in his profound way, he asked me,

"Dad, doesn't that make you feel like a relic?"

Today, I am proud that I survived my time on active duty to become a relic and show my son what I had done while serving my country in a very difficult time.

I dedicate this book to my incredible wife Monica, my son Aaron and his family.

I also wish to remember the men with whom I served who did not have the opportunity to be labelled a relic by their son.

Rest in peace my comrades.

"Things don't happen. They are made to happen."
John F. Kennedy

"Success is not the key to happiness. Happiness is the key to success. If you love what you are doing, you will be successful."

Albert Schweitzer

TABLE OF CONTENTS

"If one advances confidently in the direction of his dreams, and endeavors to live the life which he has imagined, he will meet with a success unexpected in common hours."

Henry David Thoreau

INTRODUCTION

Why is the experience I gained as a professional fighter pilot relevant to doing business and obtaining success as an entrepreneur? Because the discipline and dedication involved in both endeavors are indisputably necessary. Those things, coupled with a willingness to learn exceptional new skills and the ability to accept extreme challenges on both the body and mind, display the need for stalwart commitment.

These are only a few of the many other important components required to become an elite USAF pilot. And because of my training and education in that calling, I have had the good fortune to utilize that knowledge and allow it to guide me in each endeavor I have undertaken since. Many of the lessons I learned later in life taught me that anyone properly indoctrinated and made aware of their own life skills can adopt and learn these attitudes. It is my aim and aspiration to pass on to you those principles.

It is interesting to note that many professionals tend to surround themselves with other professionals of similar disciplines. As a result, these same professionals forget how special they are and how valuable their wisdom is to others. They may even forget how others view them, look up to them, and learn from them. This is equally true in the fighter pilot community.

As one who came from that proud community of fighter pilots, I ask you, the reader, to enjoy the stories and emotions contained within this book. And unless you have personally experienced them, many of them can only be imagined. This book is not written specifically to be a memoir, yet it is true that many of the best lessons in life are told through the events in which they actually occurred.

My belief is that as you read and re-read this book you will gain insight into your own singular and unique self. And with that insight, you will be able to successfully grow your career in whatever endeavor you may choose in your future.

"Do not let what you cannot do interfere with what you can do."
John Wooden

PROLOGUE

THE MAN IN THE FLIGHT SUIT

The air was blue with those great white puffy clouds of childhood stories. There was a feeling of the crisp morning air which was tinged with the smell of JP4 jet fuel. Taxiing along in my A-7D Corsair II jet and sitting above the pavement, atop 14,250 pounds of available thrust, I felt on top of the world.

I was strapped in to the jet with my Nomex fire resistant flight suit, my helmet which was painted in squadron colors, a g-suit, and an oxygen mask. All of this was connected in an orchestrated manner to the seat that had a ballistic charge directly beneath my butt.

The g-suit is like a pair of chaps that are tightly zippered around the legs and waist. A hose connects to an air source which inflates bladders to the suit.

The function of the g-suit is to cause a very high degree of pressure to be exerted on the legs and abdomen. This therefore helps to prevent the blood from flowing out of the upper body in the legs. This ingenious suit enables you to stay conscious while pulling up to 7+g's.

A "g" stands for gravity. The best way to explain this is for you to think of your present weight. For example, if you weigh 200 pounds at 1g—or one gravity—you are feeling your normal body of 200 pounds. But at 2g, you are feeling the equivalent to your body of 200 x 2, or 400 pounds. A 3g pull would feel like 600 pounds, and so on.

The ballistic charge under the seat is connected to a handle trigger that has the ability to shoot you and your seat up the rails and separate you from a stricken aircraft. Located in the back of the seat is a parachute that opens automatically once a separate charge blasts you apart from the seat. Of course, this is after you have been ejected from the now unmanned aircraft.

The helmet is designed to keep you from knocking yourself unconscious should you encounter turbulence that causes your head to slam against the canopy. It also prevents head injury during an egress from the aircraft. Strapped to the face of the helmet is a visor that functions to protect your eyes from wind-blasts of up to 500 mph, should you have to eject.

The oxygen mask is connected to a source of oxygen that mixes with ambient air. It is also under pressure which, when flying as high as 50,000 feet, prevents passing out from oxygen deprivation. If this pressurized oxygen should disappear, the pilot would be rendered helpless within seconds. That is because the oxygen in your lungs is expelled out due to the lack of pressure at higher altitudes. This would even apply if you were attempting to hold your breath.

"Ruckus flight, cleared for takeoff," rumbled the steady voice of the tower controller.

"Roger, Ruckus cleared for takeoff," I responded.

As we finished our checklist, with a silent hand signal to the wingman, we simultaneously lowered our canopies. Next, we armed our seats, changed our radios to tactical frequency, and turned on our Identification Friend or Foe set (IFF, for short). Our lights came on together, and we taxied in formation onto the runway.

Lining up, I gave the signal to my wingman, #2, to advance power. He nodded acceptance of the command. With a final check of the instruments and another silent signal with our heads, we released brakes together. After another quick check of the wingman and the runway ahead, we accelerated down the runway.

We reached safety check speed, and I began raising the nose slowly by pulling back on the control stick. Almost immediately, we broke free of the bonds of gravity and began our climb. I tapped my helmet with a head jerk back which signaled to the wingman to raise the gear and the flaps.

"Ruckus flight, cleared tactical," the controller said.

Then came another signal and we changed to a pre-determined battle tactical scenario with radios, IFF, and other switches. A quick waggle of the rudder pedals kicked out my wingman into loose formation. We visually looked each other over for problems, such as leaking fluids, bombs hanging improperly, and so on.

When all was satisfied and with another waggle, my wingman and I separated to 4,000 feet apart. Then, pushing over our birds, we slithered down to a battle tactical altitude of about 100 feet above the surface of the earth. This was just the beginning.

Each and every flight as a fighter pilot begins in very much the same way. Each and every time, there are hundreds of checks and re-checks, planning and executing, checking and more checking, all while working and maintaining a total sense of purpose and professionalism. Sometimes, even with all the checks, it still is not enough and someone may not come home.

The point to mention here is that an attack fighter pilot is exceptionally capable, well-trained, and disciplined. The pilot is constantly thinking of scenarios in the here-and-now as well as planning for events that will unfold in five to ten minutes in the future. And all of this is being done at speeds of up to 7+ miles per minute. As you can imagine, this requires extremely quick thinking, planning and action in order to influence the successful outcome of events up to seventy miles away.

I began thinking of all the planning and training that was ingrained in me during those years, and I realized how much these skills became useful to me in the execution of my first business. As the years of activity and success went by in my business ventures, I came to realize more and more that our breed of man—that man in the flight suit—did not need to have the advantage over someone without these skills. That is, not if I were to provide him with the tricks of the trade!

So, what are the preliminary secrets of success that become innate to the man in the flight suit? In sharing these tactics with you and in allowing them to be employed in your personal endeavors, you may begin to acknowledge and enjoy the successes that come about from them. For those of us who are properly trained are able to think ahead of the bird, both in time and in distance.

"Life has no limitations except the ones you make."

Les Brown

CHAPTER 1

A WORD ABOUT PILOTS

When I pause to reflect upon the reasons for my success within both my personal life and my business ventures, I think back to the techniques and skills I learned as a trained USAF A-7D and A-10A attack fighter pilot. How could I channel these things into all other aspects of my life with the same mission success?

Initially, I never thought about the prospects of being self-employed and certainly did not envision being an entrepreneur, but circumstances moved me in that direction. Being a single-seat jet pilot fashioned me with the skills to tread confidently through life. I later realized—after making the transition from a fighter pilot to a business entrepreneur—that my achievements were due in large part to that confidence I had gained. Life has many facets, and one very important key to success comes from how you work with that and how you control your attitude.

From having been a man both in uniform—the man in the flight suit—and a man in civilian clothes, I have come to understand the difference in perception that a uniform brings its bearer. Men in uniform have oft been revered in our society, from soldiers and military personnel to police, firemen, and doctors. Could it be that their uniform makes them stand out above the rest of society? They are different from the rest, but uniform to each other. They are the sentinels of the sectors they represent in our society.

When the uniform is removed, the sense of status seems to fade away as well, whether consciously or not. Yet, I wanted to be seen with that former perception all of the time and not just when I was in my flight suit. I wanted to continue to be that sentinel, and I realized that I could be.

You do not need to have been a single-seat attack fighter pilot nor do you need to have been in a g-suit and helmet. You can take your past successes and apply them moving forward in life in a major way with the attitude and mindset of a *man in a flight suit*!

Over the years, I have received countless letters and words of encouragement from fellow or aspiring pilots. I have combined them into three basic principles: Rules & Common Sense, Wisdom & Experience, and Ideals & Legacy.

"Adventure can be had at any time. It just depends on your state of mind."

Clive Cussler

Rules & Common Sense

1. There are Rules and there are Laws. The Rules are made by men who think that they know better how to fly your airplane than you do. The Laws, which are principles of physics, were made by the Great One. You can, and sometimes should, suspend the Rules. But you can *never* suspend the Laws.

2. The Rules are a good place to hide if you do not have a better idea or the talent to execute.

3. If you deviate from a Rule, it must be a flawless performance. For example, if you fly under a bridge, do not *hit* the bridge.

4. As an aviator in flight, you can do anything you want, as long as it is right. And we will let you know whether or not it was right after you land.

5. A tactic done twice is a procedure.

6. If you are going to fly low, do not fly slow!

"The will to win, the desire to succeed, the urge to reach your full potential . . . These are the keys that will unlock the door to personal excellence."

Confucius

Wisdom & Experience

1. He who demands everything that his aircraft can give him is a pilot; he that demands one iota more is a fool.

2. One of the most important skills that a pilot must develop is the skill to ignore those things that were designed by non-pilots to get the pilot's attention.

3. Remember that the radio is only an electronic suggestion box for the pilot. Sometimes, the only way to clear up a problem is to turn it off.

4. The only real objective of a check ride is to complete it and get the "blankety-blank" check-airman out of your airplane.

5. It never occurred to any flight examiner that the examinee could care less what the examiner's opinion of his flying ability really is.

"Quality is not an act, it is a habit."

Aristotle

Ideals & Legacy

1. The ideal pilot is the perfect blend of discipline and aggressiveness.

2. It is imperative that a pilot be unpredictable. Rebelliousness is very predictable. In the end, conforming almost all the time is the best way to be unpredictable.

3. It is a tacit yet profound admission of the pre-eminence of flying in the hierarchy of the human spirit that those who seek to control aviators via threats always threaten to take one's "wings" and not their life. I suppose that really shows which of the two is more important to an aviator.

4. If a mother has the slightest suspicion that her infant might grow up to be a pilot, she had better teach him how to put things back where he got them.

5. As a pilot, only two bad things can happen to you, and one of them will. Either 1) one day you will walk out to your aircraft knowing that it was your last flight in an

airplane, or 2) one day you will walk out to your aircraft not knowing that it will the last flight you will ever take.

6. The ultimate responsibility of a pilot is to fulfill the dreams of the countless millions of earthbound ancestors who could only stare skyward and wish.

"Choice, not chance, determines one's destiny."

Unknown

CHAPTER 2

INTRODUCING YOU TO YOU

I previously mentioned that initially the outside perception of me in my military uniform differed from the outside perception of me in my civilian clothes. What caused this change, I wondered, and more still, how could I continue not only feeling like a *man in a flight suit* but also being perceived as one? Because I realized that it was not just my skills as a fighter pilot that paved the way for my success, it was the achievements in my life prior which bolstered my confidence. And as it was with me it can also be for you, for there is nothing that you cannot do in your life and there is nothing you cannot become. Now, perhaps you may wish to know how I can make such a bold claim if I do not even know you. It is because I know that *at some point in your life, you have already achieved something*.

No matter what it was, *you have already done something significant in your life for you*. This thing, this event, occurrence or whatever 'it' was, might not have even been a noticed achievement to anyone else. But *you* know what 'it' is, and maybe it was something that you would love to tell someone about. This 'it' is your seed. It is the only one you need to have.

It is an absolute of both nature and God that all growth comes initially from a seed. In life, that seed is already within you. It already exists. So how do you grow the garden of your life? How do you reap the benefits? All you have to do is search it out, plant it, grow it, and then harvest it. And no flight suit is required.

"Believe you can, and you are halfway there."

Theodore Roosevelt

CHAPTER 3

THE SEARCH

Lessons from my Grandmother's Garden:

Early Accomplishments & Encouragement

"Don't judge each day by the harvest you reap but by the seeds that you plant."

Robert Louis Stevenson

Dig deep and way back in your memory bank and remember your first big accomplishment. The thing to keep in mind here is that there *is* something you have accomplished. Or perhaps, there are many *something*'s. For some of us, it is very obvious. For others, we may have to dig a bit deeper. This is especially true if you had an upbringing that was not particularly positive or uplifting.

Perhaps you went out for little league or tried out to be a cheerleader. You might have been asked to be in a school play, something which might have terrified you! But for some reason, you did try out for one of these things or something else similar, and you were ultimately selected for the part.

I made it on to a little league team. I also was forced to take piano lessons. What is the relevance? They both required two things: practice and persistence. You could not just show up one time and get on the team. Practice, discipline and more practice. You could not just go to the lessons in piano without practice.

Eventually, I got good enough to play regularly in baseball, and I even hit a home run. It was a very small thing in retrospect. But, then again, maybe not really so small. You see, that little victory for me meant that I could accomplish something. It was something that required me to stretch and to work beyond me by becoming something else. It allowed me to see me in a different perspective.

Learning to play piano was also like that. Even though at the time I disliked it, I kept doing it because I was disciplined to do so. Eventually, I memorized some pieces and actually got through them at a very small, public recital. What a feat that was for me at the time, to succeed at something I had once thought was just for sissies!

Are you getting the idea? Take this moment to identify some seeds of success from early on in your life. Observe the progression of these early childhood memories. For a little boy like me, it might have been winning an after-school fight or learning how to ice skate or climb a tree on my own. You see, these early victories were common place for you, weren't they?

As a child, I remember feeling that school was such a drag. I only wanted to be outside playing in the fresh air. So, being in a class room all day while sitting and trying to concentrate and focus felt like punishment to me. Yet still, there were the little achievements, such as the grades I did not think I could make or the papers I did not think I could write.

I found a paper recently, written probably when I was in 8th grade. The purpose of the paper was to write whatever came into our heads as we listened to music. Even today, I look back at that paper and like what I had written. And evidently, so did my teacher. I was encouraged.

I could run fast, as well. I remember being encouraged to run in track. And so, I did. Again, it was a little thing, but I could compete. I was also always wrestling with my brothers and sister. So, it was no big deal for me when I made the wrestling team. And I did very well. When I was fourteen, I went out after school and got a job as a bus boy at a Furr's Cafeteria. I was now making my own money, and *wow!* was that great. And again, what had I done? I had scored another little victory. I began having a veritable little pile of them for a fourteen-year-old.

I had already learned the importance of hard work, but I did not like to save money. Mom said it burned a hole in my pocket. I took that literally, I think. So, I bought stuff. One of the first items I bought was a ten-speed bicycle. I have no recollection today of what 'useful' things I did with my money, but I had a job, and that gave me a feeling of importance and self-worth.

Between my sophomore and junior year in High School, my family moved from Arvada, Colorado to Great Falls, Montana. It was very difficult to move so frequently, but then again, young people if properly encouraged can be very resilient. Mom and Dad helped my older brother and me to get summer jobs at a sheep ranch in northern Idaho. We lived in a bunk house like real cowboys.

That summer in Idaho, I learned to drive the ranch truck. It was a three-speed with a clutch and the shifter on the column. We called that a "three on a tree". I never remember telling anyone I could not do it. I just did it. I learned how to operate a very large tractor with a 10-foot cutting blade. It had little triangular blades, and whenever the blades broke, they would need replacing. I would hop off the tractor, get out my tools and a new blade and begin to replace the damaged one.

As you begin to delve in to some of your early and special memories, it is okay to forget the bad stuff. You do not need that anyway. It is not productive, and it is certainly no longer important. Your future successes are a result of you focusing on some of these positive little achievements. It may not sound like much, but believe me, these types of accomplishments are huge.

Stop now and make your list of some similar early accomplishments.

"Believe in yourself! Have faith in your abilities! Without a humble but reasonable confidence in your own powers you cannot be successful or happy."

Norman Vincent Peale

Creating Your Own Garden:

Making a List and Pulling the Weeds

"You can't build a reputation on what you are going to do!"

Henry Ford

1. What was one of your first really big achievements? What effect did it have on you?

2. What was your first athletic achievement? Did you realize at the time that it might become one of the building blocks for future successes in your life?

3. List one of your first memorable school achievements. (For me, getting C's and above on my report card meant a lot!)

4. List the first time you earned money. This does not include an allowance but rather a return of monetary reward for something you produced.

What about disappointments or personal offenses? Do these things also factor in? Of course, they do. However, if you really think about it, why should they? So many people let a single little failure, disappointment, or insult completely influence their life. It might have been some careless little remark that amounted to nothing, but some people let it mean everything. Why let someone else's inadequacies, as projected onto you via their remarks, change your wonderful life?

Let's spend just a little bit of time on this. Who were these people who negatively impacted you? Was it a casual friend or an important relative? Perhaps it was your Mom or Dad? Or, maybe it was a total nobody. Maybe it was just someone who barely passed through your life. Regardless of who they were or are, why do we allow those people control over our life? You see, you have the ability to control whether or not you allow that person's input to relegate you to a third-class position. And, it impacts everything, particularly your allowance of *their* thoughts about *you*. Get it again. Your *allowance* . . ..

You allowed . . .. So, because you allow, only allow those things which **build** you. Because ultimately, you are the best in the world at whatever you decide to do. You just need to believe that. You should really get serious about becoming your own person. Become your own unique, totally individual and beautiful person. And the way to begin believing that is for you to lock on to or anchor your other successes. A real success would be best. It could, however, even be fantasized.

Besides, regarding reality, who really knows reality? No one, not even you, knows reality. Your perception of the reality of a situation and how you accept it is the final word on the subject. That idea is worth repeating. ***Your perception of the reality of a situation and how you accept it is the final word on the subject!***

To be sure, my little successes kept me moving forward. Therefore, in your life, when you doubt yourself, let your little successes in life serve as a reminder to give you encouragement! Allow these encouragements to move you into the realm of being truly great in some particular way. It is important, however, to remember to take these victories and move to the next victory circle. Do not endlessly replay this one single incident and let it become your life. Always move forward. **Do not stagnate.**

"Always do your best. What you plant now, you will harvest later."

Og Mandino

From Concept to Reality:

Turning Early Accomplishments into Lifetime Achievements

"High expectations are the key to everything."

Sam Walton

How many people have allowed a single success to become their future by stopping there and not building onward to the next level? They become the people at the water-cooler bragging about something to everyone while never, ever doing another thing again.

So, of course, this is not the result you want. You allow this incident to define your next triumph. Let it be your next little Waterloo. Then move on. Repeat your last triumph in a new arena. Build on it!

So, how do you climb the next hurdle? First, you must move forward. Find your next mountain to climb, and then when you have doubts or inhibitions, just play back your last success!

I am astonished by how little we achieve in our life because we do not do this. We stagnate. And worse still is how easily we allow someone else to define normal or average, and then we snuggle into that little box.

We start something new and immediately we either seek to find out what is required, or we look to others to define for us what is *normal*. And rather than find our own standard, since we do not know what that is, we set our standard against others.

We are like the salesman looking around at what everyone else is selling and who is doing the best and we fit in with that standard. We attempt to beat the race times of those who are wonderful at their sport rather than going full-out at our own pace.

There are many stories of people who have entered a new field of endeavor in which success is calculated by how much or how fast a task is completed. This person, not knowing what the standard of excellence has been, is doing their job as they believe they should only to discover they are lauded as top in their department or company. And then something happens. They begin to fit into the *standard* and slide into a *normal* level, which is usually one of mediocrity. And this level is far below what they had initially accomplished.

Other examples of this might be coming into a new job and either asking what is expected in terms of production or being told what is expected. Maybe this is because there is a commission or bonus paid when a certain dollar level per month is achieved. So, this bonus level is hit and exceeded by mere pennies. What if the level was increased by 20% and this became the level required to get the bonus? Then, what seemed impossible becomes possible.

It has been said that the game of golf, since Tiger Woods began playing, has become even more competitive by being played at an even higher level. The reason? Because Tiger Woods, unlike most competitors, would only compete against himself. He would set his own standard without regard to what his competition was doing.

Another example of this would be to look at old world records that were set forty years ago. Today, they are broken fairly routinely by high school age athletes! I witnessed this personally in my life when I was selected to go to pilot training. Ever since I first became a pilot in the USAF, I have heard people tell me that that was what they truly wanted to do. Then they would offer some explanation as to why they never did.

"Well, I couldn't get accepted because of my eyes," they would say.

"Really, what was wrong with your eyes?" I would respond.

"Well, I wore glasses, and I heard that if you wore glasses, you couldn't be a pilot."

So, here it is. They decided on their own they could not qualify based on what they thought they knew but not on what they found out by actually trying.

In retrospect, it is interesting because I did wear glasses. However, prior to the requisite military eye test, I ate carrots for a week straight, and my Mom prayed for me! It did not really surprise me that I passed the requisite test, because I took it with the intent to pass it.

What is the lesson? Do not allow yourself to be the *crab in the bucket* with others who are determined to set the bar low enough that they do not ever have to achieve their greatness.

You know about the crab in the bucket, right? If not, here is the analogy. If you want a crab to stay in an open bucket, it is impossible to do that without a lid. So, what is the fix? You simply drop another crab in with the first crab. Whenever one tries to get out, the other pulls it down.

How Does Your Garden Grow:

Affecting Change in Your Environment

*"Be careful the environment you choose for it will shape you;
be careful the friends you choose for you will become like them."*

W. Clement Stone

With the *crab in the bucket* analogy in mind, I know that for me the absolute best performance I can give on anything is to be around those who encourage me. You do not want to be dragged down like a crab in a bucket. We must, absolutely must, surround ourselves with those who build us up. And in the times when you cannot, you have to find a way to change your environment to allow for this to happen.

What was your favorite subject in school? Chances are, you are doing what you do today because you excelled in something that you were encouraged in during those formative years. Sure, there are exceptions. But, even if you wanted to move into something that was of interest to you, you had to get encouragement somewhere, right? So, seek encouraging situations and people. Challenge yourself to race against yourself while moving in the direction of being encouraged by others.

Unfortunately, today many schools are staffed by negative teachers and administrators. It no longer seems that they are in the business of creating excellence. So, you will need to overcome some of the negative mindsets to which you have been exposed. This is best accomplished with the help of a coach. This coach should be someone who knows you well enough and can challenge you to do and be your best! This coach should be someone who will help you aspire to reach higher.

My first experience with this was as a cook in a very large restaurant. The owner and the head chef constantly gave me reasons to want to excel. They complimented me in ways that meant something to me. This encouraged me to rise even higher and work even harder.

But again, it is not always positive. One of my biggest challenges involved a mentor experience when I was stationed at Vance AFB in Oklahoma. The pilot training program was exceptionally demanding and challenging. This in and of itself was not necessarily negative, but the instructor who was assigned to take me from being a freshly minted officer to a skilled pilot was simply awful.

His ability to inspire confidence did not exist. He had a lackluster attitude toward me, his charge. Further, he had absolutely no desire to be an instructor pilot. Since I had not yet developed my own dreams and goals, I struggled. I did not really know myself. In retrospect, I almost allowed his poor attitude to take away the opportunity in front of me to be a jet pilot.

So, what was my solution? I decided to quit. No kidding! I did not want to work that hard for something that did not have any meaning to me. I did not aspire to be what he was. In order to quit, I was required to meet with the Chief of Training. He wanted to know why I was in pilot training in the first place. I really did not have any answer. I had never thought about it!

He proceeded to berate me. He reminded me of the difficulty of even being there. Angrily, he informed me how I was wasting the slot. There were many other men that would have loved to have had my position. He appropriately called me a wimp for my reasons and decision. Yet strangely, somehow this talk motivated me!

I began to realize that my position was really worth fighting for. Abruptly, as he was ready to throw me out, I asked him if I could possibly get another shot. To this day, I am not sure why I got another chance. It really should not have happened. He carefully explained the consequences of what I had attempted to do, and then arranged for me to be placed conditionally with another instructor.

This different instructor, Lieutenant 'Roach' Jones, was a true lover of the art of mentoring. Lt. Roach helped to change my life. He was not only a good pilot, he also made learning to fly great fun. Every day, I worked harder to not only succeed for my goal, but also to succeed for him.

I now know that this kind of mentorship and leadership is crucial to most endeavors. I strongly believe this to be true. Therefore, I suggest you force yourself to get out there and find your inspirational mentor. Work at it. As a side note, I want to point out that Lt. Roach graduated his three students at the top of the class. Thank you, Lt. Roach Jones!

Before I was given that second chance to stay on in pilot training, my goal was merely to get into the USAF. I had a pregnant wife and needed the income and benefits. Beyond that, I did not have much motivation. I had not wanted to be a pilot badly enough to be challenged by a poor mentor, because I had not made it my dream. It was not important enough for me to fight for the prize.

But now, I simply *had* to be a jet pilot. I further determined that I needed to be a fighter jock! It no longer was an option. Since I now had a true mentor who encouraged me, the work necessary to accomplish this new goal was secondary.

Was it hard work? Oh yes, definitely and beyond belief. I had not sought any challenging technical courses in college, so I had to learn all kinds of very technical skills. Mathematics, weather, flight planning, navigation, memory skills, as well as other things.

A Good Place to Grow:

Dreams and Goals

"No one can hurt you without your consent."

Eleanor Roosevelt

For most of us, a dream is a wish and a goal is a destination. Whatever you wish for is simply that. You set your goals based on your dreams. So, in identifying your goals, first think about the *perfect life for you*.

Consider areas in your life—spiritual, relationships, living arrangements, modes of transportation, how many kids you have, and so on. Based on this list, identify what you want to achieve in increments of *one* year, *five* years, and *ten* years.

For me, I have a goal to make a certain income. I then break this down into what I will have to pursue to make that income. Next, I identify the specific steps needed and the actions required to achieve those goals.

Think of it as if you are deciding to take a journey to some exotic and far-off place. If it is reachable over land, then you have choices to make. You could walk, skateboard, bicycle, drive, hitchhike, fly, or take a train. You must judge the time-frame and the distance. Obviously, you cannot possibly decide to walk if you want to go 2,000 miles and be back home within ten days! Therefore, the vehicle has to match the result.

With goals regarding income, if you have never made $250,000 per year and your present income is $75,000, you are going to have to identify some radical changes in what you are presently doing to achieve this new level. You must always be willing to make changes. Sacrifice will be part of the price.

So, now when you have the vehicle in mind, you will need to begin planning the journey step by step. Since you have identified your destination, you only need to begin! This is the key to *goal setting*. You begin by first writing down the goal and destination, then study all the elements that are required to obtain that.

We have all seen people pursue an education to be an engineer or whatever, and then they discover that not only do they not like the work, but it does not make them the income that fits their dreams.

This is the reason why coaching and mentoring are so important. You want to do what you love and enjoy and what you are called to do, but also, you want to do that which rewards you appropriately and fits your dreams.

"It is always too early to quit."

Norman Vincent Peale

CHAPTER 4

THE ROOTS

Prepare for Planting:

Faith in Your Purpose

"The quality of a person's life is in direct proportion to their commitment to excellence, regardless of their chosen field of endeavor."

Vince Lombardi

Planting your seed is all about taking what we have discussed regarding finding your past achievement and putting it in the best area to grow. In the previous chapter, we discussed the aspect of discovering your seed and laying out a plan for creating your future. So how is this ***seed planting*** accomplished?

First, we need to discover where to plant the seed. This is where the idea of faith comes in so strongly. *Faith* is a term often used to discuss spiritual or religious aspects of life. Of course, there is a spiritual aspect to creating a new you.

The faith to which I am referring is exactly like the faith which allows you to expect a crop of vegetables after planting vegetable seeds. You expect that once the seeds are planted and properly cared for, they will produce. This can be based on either your experience of this process or the knowledge of someone else's experience. So, this is the faith you need to have here. You need to understand that if you have not used this technique, you may rely on the experiences of someone else to guide you.

To work and grow, a vegetable seed does not *need* to be believed! This is also true of the *mental seed* you need to plant for your life. The seed will grow based on the nature of God's laws, just like gravity. You do not have to believe in it for it to work. The faith aspect is in taking the action and planting the seed!

Plant Your Seed:

Visualizing Your Success

"Change your thoughts and you change your world."
Norman Vincent Peale

Begin planting your seed by visualizing your success. Do this with as much reality as you can muster. See as closely as possible into your mind, as if you were actually looking at that goal for which you are aiming . . ..

Long before I became interested in reading for personal improvement and development, I occasionally had the need to visualize. *Visualization* is a process of seeing in your mind the desired result before you have experienced it in the present, or physical, realm.

Having made it through pilot training, water survival, basic mountain and winter survival, advance fighter training, then four months of specialty training in the very complex single-seat attack fighter, the A-7D, I hit a wall. One of the requirements for successful completion of the course was to refuel behind an airborne tanker at night. If we did not do it at least once, we would be washed out of the program. We were allowed only two attempts.

We were already able to do this during the day, so it should have been a pretty easy process to do the same thing at night in the dark. The difference in this case, however, happened to be the instructor much more so than the event.

There were three students and one instructor. The instructor happened to be a very angry and arrogant senior squadron commander. His method of encouragement was to begin uttering obscenities well before we even got close to the tanker.

"You idiots, we are getting ready to wash you out as fighter pilots, so let's go up and get this over with," he would say.

I had to overcome his lack of faith and create my own. Somewhere, I had heard that you could *arm chair* fly a mission. *Arm chair flying* is another way of saying to visualize. I like this term because it sounds more logical than *visualization*.

It is sitting in a chair and, in your mind, flying the entire mission from that spot. I determined this was going to be a very important flight the next day. I was not ready to give up and roll over. So, I decided to try this suggested technique, which was basically just going through the motions of a future planned event.

The goal of this is to see every aspect of the event, its potential dilemmas, and hurdles, and then see yourself dealing with these potential problems in advance before you actually deal with them in reality.

To think through a flight and see every detail of the flight from takeoff to landing was new to me. However, I was told by an instructor to try doing this. So, I took the action and did exactly that. Three times, for over two hours each time, I visualized my flight the next night. That was my method of studying. I *saw* every aspect of the flight.

The next evening, the same flight of four sleek A-7D aircraft sped down the runway and steadily increased to 120 miles per hour before lifting off. Within seconds, we reached nose rotation speed. Pulling back on the control stick, my aircraft began ever so gently to achieve a 12-degree nose-up attitude. As soon as we did, we were air-borne. Flying in formation, the lights of my fighter gently caressed the night air.

The flight leader signaled gear up, flaps up, and power back. Kicking me from close formation to route, or extended formation, we began to wait for our other flight element of two aircraft to join us. About three minutes later, we had them in formation and began to set up on the climb to the pre-planned flight route.

Forty minutes later, we reached the area to rendezvous with the flying gas station and were cleared in to join up with the tanker. Being a very dark night, it was easy to pick out this mammoth flight monster. It was a KC-135 and was all lit up like a giant flying Christmas tree.

Our flight lead screamed some obscenities at us, saying he wanted to get his gas before his rookies crashed into the tanker and kept him dry, or without fuel. Of course, all these intimidations no longer carried any weight with me, as I had already seen myself doing this very successfully many times within the past twenty-four hours from my chair.

And it proved successful. Along with the other two student pilots, we got our gas without further incident.

Nurture the Seedling:

Realizing Your Goal

"Be a yardstick of quality. Some people aren't used to an environment where excellence is expected."
Steve Jobs

The point is, when *realizing* your goal, you must remember the following things:

1. See yourself doing *successfully* whatever it is you plan to accomplish;

2. Practice, practice, and practice some more;

3. Never doubt yourself, and;

4. Above all, take action! Even the smallest action will empower you and move you forward. You cannot steer a parked car. Likewise, you cannot take off in an airplane until you apply power. The defining attribute to action is motion. Move forward now, this very minute. **Let your preparation become your initial action**.

Failures in our minds are like poison, but the repetition of our successes is the antidote. And the only way to do that is to keep getting up and going at it again. Be the success you were designed to be.

"Affirmation without discipline is the beginning of delusion."

Jim Rohn

CHAPTER 5

THE GROWTH

Growing Good Crops:

Decide to be the Best

"Can you imagine what I would do if I could do all I can?"
Sun Tzu

Whatever business endeavor you choose to undertake or be part of, make it your prerogative to be the best. Do not just be *above average* or *good* at something. Be the greatest! How do you do this? Simply decide to label yourself as the greatest. And as you admit it to yourself and to others, several very important things will begin to happen.

Firstly, you are admitting it to you! This element alone can cement the thought in your mind and within your core which is your confident belief of your expert status. This will then translate itself into everything you do. Your actions then become motivated by this inner knowledge and confidence.

And secondly, when you talk with others, who may or may not be an expert in anything, they will respect your positioning of yourself. To them, you represent in life that which they would appreciate having for themselves.

Being genuinely good at something is truly rare and remarkable. Try to think for a moment of someone you have met in your life who was an expert at something. Now try remembering if you ever met someone who was known by themselves or others as the *best*.

These same people, by their proximity to you, find themselves in the company of an expert and thereby gain a bit of their own notoriety and confidence. It is the excitement of being able to tell people that they met an expert in the field of

_____.

Another big part of *growing it* is having *faith*. You wouldn't plant a tomato seed in the ground and either not expect the seed to grow or expect it to grow something besides tomatoes. People often do what they need to be doing, but they doubt their actions, thus spoiling the crop. If you have faith in your actions and do not doubt your work, you can certainly expect the correct results.

When Not All Seeds Sprout:

Reversing Setbacks and Failure

> *"When written in Chinese, the word 'crisis' is composed of two characters. One represents danger and the other represents opportunity."*
>
> John F. Kennedy

The process of *visualization*—which follows through all your steps—is a good element to firmly entrench in your habits. Why? Because you *will* have setbacks. You *will* have little defeats. And yes, you *will* have the occasional failure! So perceptibly, we start to see the failures when we attempt to move forward. This can almost certainly lead to another failure. And then, that scenario becomes the new reality.

If this has happened, it can assuredly be reversed. However, you must begin to exercise a different mindset. You must exercise one in which you only allow yourself to see the event you are beginning with a successful conclusion.

Remember, you can begin to create your own reality. The reality which you are creating must begin with you seeing the successful completion of an event. I recommend you to do this multiple times per day in different ways.

Further, become your own cheerleader. Talk things out with yourself. Hear your voice commending you on your victory. Self-affirmation is important to us all. Guard your thoughts and mind from ever admitting anything less than perfection. It is better to not say anything if you cannot prevent yourself from speaking defeat or negativity. Flee from gossipers. Do not allow yourself to be anywhere in which you can be mentally soiled.

Nurturing Your Seedlings:

Positively Affirm Your Aspirations

"Words are magical in the way they affect the minds of those who use them."

Aldous Huxley

One of the analogies of this book dwells on the Biblical principles of seed time and harvest. If you have ever grown a garden, you know that there are basic elements to a garden. A gardener never plants just one seed. Further, you want to always guard and protect your new fragile plant. Since you planted it, you want it to grow. Therefore, guard and protect it. Water it, weed it, and tend to it.

If you have developed a habit of negative talk or being around negative talk, change your environment. But you will have to work at it. And I do mean really work. An immediate requirement to change this habit is to write down a dozen *affirmations* on a card. These affirm the goals you wrote earlier. But they also may contain specific traits and habits that support your overall well-being.

Carry them with you and read them out loud to yourself multiple times per day. The more you do it the better. Put a copy in the visor of your car, and every time you start your car, pull them down and recite them out loud. Reading them with great regularity is very important.

Write down affirmations that are a positive reflection of what you desire or what it is that you seek to change. Make it just like you are reading a checklist. For a fighter pilot, that *man in the flight suit*, this is standard practice. As a pilot, I would read my checklist aloud, step-by-step, to make sure that we accomplished every required, and perhaps seemingly mundane, point. One could easily forget things and that forgetfulness could easily and quickly kill you. In an airplane with a crew of two pilots, this reading was accomplished with a *challenge and response technique*. This is something you can do with your spouse when you drive, also.

This makes your affirmations take on an even bigger significance and relevance. However, in a single-seat environment, you must concentrate and focus on the points. So, try this: **focus on what you are saying as you are saying them, and see it coming true**.

Therefore, a *checklist in your car*, which are your affirmations, are a true reflection of a pilot's normal routine.

> *"Any idea, plan, or purpose may be placed in the mind through repetition of thought."*
>
> Napoleon Hill

Sample Checklist of Positive Affirmations

1. I am an expert in my personal endeavors.

2. I am in great health! (Say this even if you don't feel well. The mind is powerful!)

3. I enjoy phenomenal success in all areas of my life.

4. I have an incredible spouse.

5.   I have beautiful children.

6.   I make $30,000 per month.

7.   I have loving friends who look up to me.

8.   I am a capable leader.

9.   I am an inspirational teacher.

10.   I have tremendous energy.

11.   I am enthusiastic and full of natural excitement.

The secrets of effective self-talk should include what you want to have as if you already possess it. It should therefore always be in the present tense. It is best to be repeated aloud. You should say it with as much conviction as you can muster until it becomes easier to say, naturally and with gusto.

Benefits include, but are not limited to, effectively changing your outlook on the day and in your life as well as perpetrating the actions necessary to put you on autopilot. That is correct, autopilot. Your mind and your actions will begin to automatically drive you forward in the directions you have set for yourself.

Everything about our lives is traceable to our beliefs and perceptions. We quite literally are in charge of creating ourselves. If you only accept the notion of this, without even totally embracing the concept, you will move forward.

The last couple of direct things I will say about affirmations relates to an experience I had while preparing for my Federal Aviation Administration (FAA) Airline Transport Pilot (ATP) test. I had completed my obligation with the USAF and was preparing for a possible career with commercial airlines. The ATP test is a very long and exhaustive test. The average pass score after studying for months is 73%. And this is usually on a second attempt.

I had purchased a study course and sat through two days of intensive training. Interestingly, the first thing they taught was how to study. It violated everything I had ever learned about preparation. We were told to read out loud while writing down what we were reading. The principle was that our brains would learn and retain more if we were using more of our senses. I found this to be reliable advice that brought anticipated results, for it is true that reading aloud while you are writing uses four of your senses. Ultimately, I ended up passing on the first try with a 93%.

The other experience was when I gave my first talk which was in front of about eighty people. I knew the material. But by rehearsing the talk out loud, I became comfortable with the material. I cemented in my mind how I would present that material and what emphasis I would place on which points.

If you can cement in your mind what you do want, you can also experience cementing things in your brain that you do not want there, such as: "*I am starting to feel a cold coming on . . ..*" or "*I just don't think I have what it takes to do that . . ..*" These are very counterproductive statements to make. And while it is bad enough to think it, it is worse to affirm it by saying it out loud.

Pulling the Weeds:

Removing Things that Stifle Growth

> "*A man who wants to lead the orchestra must turn his back on the crowd.*"
>
> Max Lucado

You must tend to your seed and your crop to assure a harvest. You cannot allow the weeds of *failure thought* to enter your brain. Success is an attitude, and it takes full time work and concentration. It takes work at controlling and programming. There is no luck involved with people who are successful. They have programmed and controlled their futures through their minds and attitudes.

Think of these elements while you are reading. When I mentioned earlier to flee from gossipers, I meant that you should use the commonsense approach of protecting the soil and the seed. You would not expect to gain much of a harvest if you routinely poured bleach on your ground. In fact, you would very well kill your plant. Every aspect of your successful journey must be viewed with this kind of concern and caution.

Take responsibility! Be able to accept that you are the reason you are where you are presently. This all comes from your thoughts, your actions, your speech, your attitude, and your preparedness. Belly up and take responsibility for you. Avoid the blame game.

Don't be lazy! Why should you have to be motivated by some external source or person to move you forward? Of course, we all want to say we are the greatest and rely on excuses to let us off the hook. Rather than put yourself down, look at what you have or have not done in the pursuit of your goals and dreams and make the proper corrections.

Have you ever watched a video of a missile being launched from a plane at the target? If it is a moving target, as life is, then the missile is constantly leading the target slightly and is also constantly making the corrections necessary to hit the target. A splash on the target is a result of hundreds of course corrections.

It does matter where you are aiming. Be sure of the target, lock in on it, and then with total and absolute concentration and focus, stay moving toward the goal. Make the corrections, but never give up on the prize.

Providing Good Nutrients for Growth:

Holistic Choices for a Healthy Life

"Discipline is the bridge between goals and accomplishment."

Jim Rohn

Holistic life involves many aspects. Time and space do not allow for details of all of them here, so I will mention the effective basics. It is a **concentration on being** involved in all areas of your life. Any one of them can cause you to fail.

Health

This is an easy deal that ties in to self-affirmation. You should work to spend time taking care of the body God has given you.

When you are injured and/or sick, this becomes a major focus in your life, and all else is relegated to minor importance. But if you stay proactive in your health, the things that impede good health may be prevented.

There are two secrets to achieving this:

1. Be proactive and not reactive. Do not let a doctor figure out your needs. You know your body better than anyone. Educate yourself on a healthy regimen. Include in that regimen a positive attitude, whole-foods nutrition, and spinal alignment. (Check out: Health in a Fighter Pilot's World and Fighter Pilot in the Kitchen.)

2. Stay in motion. Yes, you can go to a gym or a work-out facility. However, if you lack the necessary time in your day, at least start each day with a stretching routine. Do this within the first five or ten minutes after waking. These few minutes will help you to become focused and alert to take on the day, and they may drastically improve your morning attitude and prevent injuries during the physical demands of the day. You will also gently increase your metabolic and heart rates which can help you maintain a healthy weight and shape. Walk or ride a bike four or more times per week.

Relationships

The health of your relationships has either a positive or negative influence on whatever it is you are attempting to do. Again, be proactive and never reactive. It is very hard to get back to a place where you are comfortable if you let this get away from you.

Financial Concerns

You cannot allow yourself to be distracted. If you cannot deal with the major effects of the financial concerns in your life, your missile will not make it to your target. You cannot allow yourself to get behind financially. But sometimes you will, and if/when you do, you must fight your way back to the top. It is inevitable that we experience the tides of life. Sometimes, the tide is in and sometimes it is out. You must try to minimize when the tide is out and maximize when it is in. But regardless, you have to battle your way back. Remember, it is fruitless to participate in the blame game or to justify that everyone else is in the same boat or that there are good reasons and excuses for your situation. These things are totally immaterial. Simply do not accept the present as your permanent reality. Be proactive to change your temporary predicament.

Spiritual/Emotional

Your spiritual and emotional life is completely intertwined with your whole or holistic well-being. A focused energy toward a daily and weekly routine in worship and reflection are essential. Again, it is crucial to be proactive instead of reactive.

> *"Self-suggestion makes you master of yourself."*
> W. Clement Stone

These four areas above in no way constitute an entire list. But each of these are major areas of life. It is essential to take this abbreviated list and expand your thoughts on what is required in action for you to work on these items.

Other areas to consider at any age or station in life

1. Leisure;

2. Volunteering within the community, and;

3. Career, income, and the rewards of work. I am sure you have heard it said that your perfect job or business would be one that you would do without pay.

Earlier, I wrote about the process of *goal setting*. There is much that is written about and lectured upon regarding goal setting. Remember though, a goal is like a target. Why would you launch expensive missiles at a non-target? Why would you shoot at something that does not exist? Furthermore, why would you continue to endlessly spend money on attending schools for a 'piece of paper' you may or may not ever use in the hopes of ascertaining a direction in life? You should avoid getting deeply into debt for this piece of paper and be clear about the rewards before you invest heavily in a degree that might never be an adequate return on your investment, both in time and money. Just because you get the paper does not mean that the job or career could not have been had without it.

Many of you might be able to point fingers at your own life and know what I am talking about. We are sometimes less than certain about which priorities to set in our lives to determine our end-result. So, someone tells us to get out there and get a degree and then we go looking for a job that fits the degree we were awarded. But perhaps we worked backwards doing this and went through the motions without ever even knowing how much the desired job will pay, where we will live, or how much time we will have left over to 'live' our life. Determine how you want your life to look.

Selecting the Crops:

Target the End Result

"When it is obvious that the goals cannot be reached, don't adjust the goals, adjust the action steps."

Confucius

Jot down some thoughts about your target or goal so that you may begin firing your missiles at the prize. You can then make the corrections to do what you will and *not* what is left over for you to do.

Again, take responsibility and do not make excuses. If you wanted to be a fighter pilot, why didn't you? Why *don't* you? Is it really too late?

When flying as a flight lead, there would be many elements that would go into a mission. We would first get scheduled a flight time and learn the number of jets that would be in the flight. Next, the pilots' names and the aircraft tail numbers were assigned. Each pilot would be assigned his position in the flight based on experience.

Lead was always number one but not necessarily because he had the most rank or flight time. The leader that day might have gained experience with other more experienced pilots in the formation. Typically, there were two elements of two planes. Each element had responsibility within the formation of four. *Lead* would also accept the assigned mission for the day's flight. In peace time, this would usually be a simulated combat flight to a bombing range. Sometimes it would also involve other dissimilar types of aircraft.

In a Search and Rescue (SAR) mission, this would involve the 'gas station in the sky' refueling tanker, 'jolly green' rescue helicopters, and other fighter support. A forward air controller (FAC) would designate—identify and point out—the survivor. The SAR Leader, also known as "Sandy", would locate and authenticate the survivor on the ground in hostile enemy territory.

This was a very complex mission, and it would take enormous amounts of time and energy to plan. However, you could not always guarantee that there was going to be time. Sometimes the time of a survivor staying free of capture was minimal, and sometimes it was not. Therefore, the success of the mission meant to always be ready. Preparedness was the key. Even so, essential elements of the pre-flight briefing would entail times, fuel considerations, ordinances, weather-related and hostile-forces scenarios, as well as abort procedures, low fuel, and safe flight areas. You would plan and discuss the applicable rules of engagement, also known as ROI, for the mission type, minimum flight altitudes, call signs, and so on.

No matter how well planned you might be, the fluidity of the mission and the exigencies of the ever-changing battle plan forced a flight to constantly be able to adapt and change, always within the confines of the discipline of the leader.

It is important to mention, however, that in all cases, it was not enough to just order people around. You had to exude confidence, make rational decisions, and keep everything flowing forward. In life, we get the luxury of thinking that we can always back off, take a break, sit down, relax, and entertain ourselves. In reality, can you really do this when there is so much at stake? You should be constantly thinking of how you can fulfill your mission plan, be it daily, weekly, monthly, and yearly. However, even if you have a well-written plan, you still should be flexible. Flexibility in flight is as important as being flexible in arriving at the successful achievement of your goals.

A very important aspect to the flight's success also went into the extensive planning. It was a very focused and busy time before the flight, one which could make the flight either a success or less than a success on the mission, or even a disaster. If you had the luxury of planning the flight over several days, that would allow for even more studying and planning.

Eventually, the scheduled time came when action had to commence. The planning was over. It was time to take off and go toward the mission. It is all very similar in life to what we need to do. Your life's planning and then movement toward your dreams and goals requires this attention and preparedness for whatever eventuality.

In life, there is this comparison. There is a time of intense focus. My challenge to you is to focus with intense concentration several times each week, and just as if you were preparing for a flight, allow a one-hour block of time to do this. Focus completely, without the distractions inherent in your office or work environment which might pull you away. If you do this exercise at home, prepare your area to be free of distractions. If you do it in office environment, put a 'Do Not Disturb' sign on your door or cubicle. *The important thing is to mentally and physically engage your creative energy towards the mission or goal you have set.*

"The truest wisdom is a resolute determination."

Napoleon

CHAPTER 6

THE HARVEST

What does it mean to harvest your crop? Think of a farmer on a combine out cutting and threshing. They leave the crop sitting in the fields for a while, and then eventually, the farmer comes and collects the harvest. The farmer puts it in some sort of storage facility, and then it goes off to market.

From identifying and planting your seed, to growing it, and now finally to harvesting, activity in life never stops. We should remember that part of what is accomplished in harvesting a farm crop is the retention of seed for the next planting. **The harvest is not an end but a cycle which is oriented around a new beginning**.

Picking the best seed from your life, selling off the harvest of the rest of your crop, and then preparing the ground for the next year is an essential element of your existence. Look at what you have accomplished in the pursuit of your goals, reexamine the good things and learn from the bad, and then reset your new goals.

When setting your new goals, be careful not to constrict or contract your mind set. Occasionally when we have the inevitable setbacks, the temptation is to ease back into the known comfort zone. We might include tightening our belt financially. And while it is certainly responsible to live within our means and our budget, be very careful that you do not slip backwards in your thinking.

Attack life! The best defense is a strong, powerful, and even willful offense. No matter when or where you are in your life, whatever you have or have not accomplished, it is always time to stop on occasion and evaluate the condition in which you find yourself. Then, prepare yourself anew for the next set of challenges and get excited about going forward.

"Dreams come true. Without that possibility, nature would not incite us to have them."

John Updike

CONCLUSION

In the Bible, there is a very powerful message relayed by one of the writers:

"Give thanks in all things."

When you think of this, you should never get upset or angry about anything. There is a definite benefit, seen or unseen, which has occurred. When I was in the process of writing these last few pages, I went to the Phoenix airport to pick up a very special person, and when I went back to where the car was parked, I simply could not find it. We were delayed late into the evening for at least forty minutes while I stumbled around looking for and finally asking for help.

I was sure of the message and benefit that occurred here. Maybe it was forcing us to work together to solve this problem. Maybe it was in preparing myself to make a note of my position in the parking lot somewhere. Or maybe, in those minutes I spent bumbling around, a major accident was avoided.

Each day hands us little opportunities. Sometimes, they look like insurmountable obstacles and hurdles. Some of them hurt us and mar us emotionally. Yet, we need to see each of these for what they are and allow them the benefit of moving into our life in the most positive way possible.

In doing this, we are preparing our fields for the seeds we will plant in them, and this will determine the new crop and its health and the future foundations of our well-being and success in life! Finally, make your life the one you want it to be. Be the *man in the flight suit*! And always bear in mind, you are the one ultimately in control of flying your plane.

"Don't be afraid of your worst times. If you learn from them, you'll look back on them as your best times."

Robert Kiyosaki

"Once the wings go on, they never come off, whether they can be seen, or not. It fuses to the soul through adversity, fear and adrenaline, and no one who has ever worn them with pride, integrity and guts, can ever sleep through the 'call of the wild' that wafts through bedroom windows in the deep of the night.

"When a good pilot leaves the 'job' and retires, many are jealous, some are pleased and yet others, who may have already retired, wonder. We wonder if he knows what he is leaving behind, because we already know.

"We know, for example, that after a lifetime of camaraderie that few experience, it will remain as a longing for those past times.

"We know in the world of flying, there is a fellowship which will last long after the flight suits are hung up in the back of the closet. We know even if he throws them away, they will be on him with every step and breath that remains in his life.

We also know how the very bearing of the man speaks of what he was and, in his heart, still is."

Author Unknown

ABOUT THE AUTHOR

Major Accomplishments Business

- Owner – www.FighterPilotintheKitchen.com – physical product business
- Past President – International Orthodox Christian Charity – operating 24 retail bookshops (United Kingdom)
- Owner/Developer – Network Marketing business – responsible for training and coaching hundreds of aspiring, new franchise business owners
- Organizer/Speaker Trainer for major events attended by thousands
- District Manager – major fast food restaurant chain
- Owner/Developer – 9 store restaurant chain

Professional Pilot Roles

- Combat trained attack/fighter pilot, flying the A-7D Corsair II, and later the A-10A Warthog
- USAF Formal Course Instructor Pilot Civilian contract instructor pilot Royal Saudi Air Force in F15C aircraft simulator – Taif, Saudi Arabia
- Range Safety Supervisor – Khamis Mushayt, Saudi Arabia
- Range Control Officer - Gila Bend, Arizona
- Captain – international airline

Phil received his Bachelor's Degree in History and Aerospace Studies – Southern Illinois University, Edwardsville Campus.

Phil is married, has a son, and three grandchildren.

Phil Brewer

Pilot, Entrepreneur, Consultant

Author of:

Fighter Pilot in the Kitchen

Effective Communications

Changes, the Book

www.PhilBrewer.com

From <u>Effective Communications: The Fighter Pilot's Guide</u>

"As we learn how to evolve within our world, it is easy to feel lost in the maze. We are moving at blinding speeds, and the traditional values and roles of men and women are becoming increasingly blurred. This has caused a tremendous amount of confusion within our society.

Just as a fighter pilot has to adapt to his fast-paced environment, we too must learn strategies for survival. Our communications with each other are crucial. We must teach ourselves to utilize these tried and true methods, in order to be successful, respectful, well-adjusted members of society."

My wonderful friend and wife, Monica.

Reviews for <u>Doing Business Like a Fighter Pilot: G Suit and Helmet Not Required</u>

"A short and clear exposition of the principles and practices of a successful jet pilot and how to apply those practices and principles to all of life. It will help you get off the ground and fly."

William Ophuls – author of <u>Immoderate Greatness</u>, <u>Why Civilizations Fail</u>, <u>Sane Polity</u>, <u>A Pattern Language</u>, <u>Plato's Revenge: Politics in the Age of Ecology</u>, and many fine other books

"What an inspiring book! I like the pace and all the allusions to flying. Like the way you lifted off with... 'breaking free of the bonds of gravity we begin our climb...' You've got many more memorable quotes: 'The Rules are a good place to hide if you don't have a better idea and the talent to execute it.' Or: 'One of the beautiful things about a single pilot aircraft is the quality of the social experience.' The advice is right on – recognizing achievements regardless of their size and not letting a little put-down throw one off course; don't allow the weeds of failure thoughts, etc... The crab in the bucket analogy is absolutely true."

William Cates – author of <u>The Unlimited Salad Bar</u>, and other entertaining books

"Being able to heed the wisdom of real-world people and their experiences is paramount to personal growth. And sometimes, all we need is a bit of common sense and straight talk to get us there. Phil's book offers just that within his exciting scope of expertise. His personal anecdotes, though mainly specific to military and aviation, are relatable, and their lessons warrant great value for anyone."

Rachel J. Beard – author, screenwriter, and editor

"Get this book! Thanks Phil, for your support and service to our Country."

Coach Ron Tunick – author of <u>The Thinking Room</u>; president of Nations Transaction Services, and; radio personality

"Phil is an incredibly inspiring figure who stands out starkly against the bleak landscape of modernity. In this book, he takes timeless wisdom to new heights for any reader. The result is an absolute joy, whether you need a shove or just a nudge toward positive thinking."

Mark Brewer – founding partner of Brewer & Pritchard P.C.

www.ingramcontent.com/pod-product-compliance
Lightning Source LLC
Chambersburg PA
CBHW021008180526
45163CB00005B/1935